Meet the Challenges of Working as a Doctor

Books for Doctors

Susan Kersley

Published by Susan Kersley, 2025.

While every precaution has been taken in the preparation of this book, the publisher assumes no responsibility for errors or omissions, or for damages resulting from the use of the information contained herein.

MEET THE CHALLENGES OF WORKING AS A DOCTOR

First edition. July 1, 2025.

Copyright © 2025 Susan Kersley.

ISBN: 979-8223512790

Written by Susan Kersley.

Table of Contents

1. Why you should read this book.

Are you an overworked doctor, neglecting life's pleasures for professional success? Do you define that success in your own way?

Despite your successful medical career and recognition, do you feel a sense of incompleteness?

Do you feel guilty about gradually realising there is more to life than Medicine?

What is it about the culture of Medicine that means many doctors believe everything else in life must take second place to their progress in their specialty?

Many senior doctors refuse to acknowledge past mistakes. Therefore, they insist complete dedication to a medical specialty is essential for success.

Is that true?

When you are passionate about what you do, you will be involved in it for many, if not all, of your waking hours. You must balance patient care, research, reading journals, and reflection.

When you return to work after an evening out, or a week away on holiday, you feel energised, refreshed and ready to deal with whatever medical emergencies, or patient's dilemmas your day brings, with new enthusiasm.

When you are desperately overworked, you may consider swimming or cycling counterintuitive.

I challenge you to do something which takes you away from the medical workplace for a few hours and notice the positive effect doing this regularly has on your energy, motivation and your interaction with patients.

2. Why I wrote this for you.

Every day there are more articles about how stressed doctors are, how the workload is increasing and how many doctors are considering leaving the medical profession because they are suffering from burnout and stress.

I know what it's like to have endless demands made on you and your time and to feel as though you will never get to the end of the work.

I know what it's like to juggle too many plates and to be unsure which ones will fall. Too often, that means neglecting not only your family and friends but also your own needs for rest and relaxation.

Imagine having a perfect work-life balance between your life as a doctor and the rest of your life so you have a fulfilling and successful life practising Medicine while also devoting enough time to your partner, your family and friends and your own interests and hobbies while also looking after your own health and well-being.

You may think of many ways you could achieve this, and it's worth reflecting on what you have tried already.

If there's a gap in your life between how it is and how you want it to be, then the way to fill it is step by step.

3. Challenges of working as a doctor.

Of all the things that you, like many doctors, may find most challenging is being able to balance medical work with the rest of your life. You want to be a doctor who is above reproach, so find it difficult to say no.

Each day you are bombarded by requests to see this patient, sort out that problem, answer a telephone call, give an opinion about a situation, while you are trying to get through your work and concentrate on the matter at hand. These distractions which can drain your energy, use time, make your life less balanced and cause you to feel frustrated and exhausted.

Here are some challenges you may face:

Long hours and burnout: You work extended hours, including nights and weekends. These demanding schedules can lead to physical and mental exhaustion, increasing the risk of burnout.

Emotional strain: You often deal with life-and-death situations, which can take a significant emotional toll. You must manage your own feelings while providing support to patients and their families during difficult times.

Keeping up with medical advances: The medical field is constantly developing. You must commit to lifelong learning to stay updated on the latest research, treatments, and technologies, which can be overwhelming.

Patient demands and expectations: Patients increasingly expect immediate responses and high-quality care. Managing these expectations and providing compassionate care is challenging, especially with limited resources.

Administrative burden: You face overwhelming paperwork and administrative responsibilities, which can detract from the time you spend with patients. Balancing clinical duties with administrative tasks can lead to frustration.

Dealing with insurance and legal issues: Navigating the complexities of healthcare insurance and the fear of malpractice lawsuits can add stress. This often leads to defensive medicine, where you may order unnecessary tests to protect yourself legally.

Work-life balance: The demanding nature of the profession can make it difficult for you to find a balance between work and personal life. This can strain relationships and lead to decreased job satisfaction.

Staffing issues: Many healthcare facilities face staffing shortages, which can lead to increased workloads for you and decreased quality of care for patients.

Cultural and language barriers: Treating a diverse patient population may present challenges in communication and understanding cultural differences, which are essential for providing effective care.

Ethical dilemmas: You may encounter ethical dilemmas in your practice, such as end-of-life decisions, resource allocation, and balancing patient independence with clinical judgment.

Each of these challenges can affect your ability to deliver optimal care while maintaining your own well-being.

Working as a doctor can be overwhelming. You want to learn everything and gain experience as much as possible.

There is constant pressure to study for more qualifications, to investigate every patient as fully as you can, to do everything in preference to your own needs.

MEET THE CHALLENGES OF WORKING AS A DOCTOR

The need to look after yourself takes a back seat easily. Medicine becomes like an ever-hungry monster eating you up. You become obsessed with wanting to be perfect and to achieve this. You keep on going even when you are hungry, exhausted, and you have done nothing except work and sleep, for days on end. You may have forgotten how important self-care is. Perhaps you've put your own needs aside and let those of the demands of your work take over most of your life.

You know, deep down, this is not an acceptable state of affairs, but you carry on because you believe you have no choice. Stress affects those who could make a difference just as much as it affects you.

However, you really need to eat more healthily, get enough sleep and take more exercise. You are human, like everyone else. Your own health and well-being depend on you looking after yourself. Your ability to find the perfect balance between Medicine and life will depend on recognising how important your needs are and how your life improves when you address these.

4. Get your boundaries clear.

Become very sure about what you will or won't do and learn how to say 'no' in an assertive rather than an aggressive way.

There are things that only you can and must do, but there are many requests that others, whether they are patients or colleagues, ask of you that you may feel pressure to do, but they are not your responsibility, and it is fine to refuse. The sooner you say 'no', the better.

You might have agreed to help a colleague as a favour, only to discover that they expect you to continue, past your agreed-upon time.

Don't expect others to be mind-readers. Stop getting frustrated if colleagues, nurses, or secretaries don't understand what you want them to do. Maybe you've made assumptions and haven't been precise about what you are expecting from them. Take a few deep breaths and explain, calmly, what you will or won't do, from now on.

Start practicing saying 'no' without sounding apologetic or giving lots of excuses. Each time you say 'I can't do that because I have to...' you are opening yourself up to the counterargument of suggestions about how you could do both.

If you want to change your life, an important principle is that life can be as simple as changing your personal boundaries.

Your boundaries are what you will put up with or tolerate before you say 'stop.' How much more will you put up with before you say 'no' or 'enough is enough'?

⬦ Where do you draw the line around yourself?

⬦ Who defines your personal boundary, you or someone else?

At what point do you say 'I will not put up with this any longer' and mean it? Too often, other people define where their boundaries are and expect you to agree. Clearly define your personal boundaries; for example, if you must leave work at a certain time, decide what tasks can wait until tomorrow to maintain that boundary.

When you have effective boundaries, you will be able to:

◇ Say 'no' to things which aren't a priority.

◇ Recognise what someone else can do.

◇ Understand you can do some things less often.

◇ Recognise that some tasks are unnecessary.

Decide which of your boundaries must change and tell the others, affected by your change, what you have decided. State your intention assertively, without getting involved in discussion, just say 'this is what I'm going to do.'

When you do this, your life will change.

It's important to establish clear boundaries with your patients to maintain a professional relationship and protect your wellbeing.

Here are some tips to get your boundaries clear:

Make it specific what your role involves, and what patients can expect from you. This means setting expectations around what you can and cannot do for your patients, as well as what you expect from them.

- Communication is key to setting boundaries. Be direct in your communication with patients and don't be afraid to say 'no' when necessary.
- Consistency is important for boundaries. Make sure you are

applying it in relation to your boundaries to all your patients and colleagues and that you are not making exceptions for certain individuals.

- Be aware of your limitations. This means knowing when you are overworked and need a break, and when to refer a patient to a colleague.
- It's okay to seek support from colleagues or a mental health professional if you are struggling with setting boundaries. You are not alone, and seeking help is a sign of strength.   By setting clear boundaries, you can establish a professional relationship that is positive for both parties. This can lead to better patient outcomes and a more fulfilling career as a doctor.

5. Is it inevitable?

You probably work excessive hours, leaving you little time for outside interests. One of the most common challenges is managing your time effectively.

When you aren't time aware, the work seems to be endless and takes priority over the rest of your life. This means that your work-life balance suffers. The less you manage your time, the more the problem grows.

This affects your life outside of work too. Not only does it affect your friends and family, but also the relationship with your partner.

Most crucial of all is the effect on your health and well-being, because when you cannot manage your time successfully, your personal, physical and emotional health suffers.

A choice of either 'forget the rest of your life' or leave Medicine?

Has being overworked turned into part of the medical culture? Perhaps it has for those doctors who survive by turning to drink or eating too much as a way of managing the stress of too much to do. Others decide to leave the profession.

If you leave work late and take tasks home with you every evening and weekend, remind yourself that you are not superhuman and you are like everyone in your need of rest and relaxation.

You need some time away from work to enjoy sport and hobbies, being with your partner, friends and family and also time for yourself and your own self-care. If you neglect these, then your health, both physical and emotional, suffers and affects the way you care for your patients. If you go into your workplace to catch up at the weekend, even when you aren't on call, then you need to act sooner rather than later to stop this way of life. It is possible to find your personal prescription for change and have a life.

You probably have too much to do each day. You may believe there is nothing you can do about this situation and it's just the way things are. But this isn't so.

Here are some of the biggest mistakes you may be making. Stop these and your life will change too.

You agree to do whatever anyone asks of you: 'No' is a small word which has a powerful effect. When asked to do something extra, try saying 'no'. 'Will you see another three patients in your clinic today?' 'Can I interrupt you while you are seeing patients even for something which could wait?' There will always be times when an emergency means that 'yes' is the answer. But most things can wait.

You setting boundaries and do not keep to them. Others might persuade you to see more patients than you planned, even if you set a patient limit and avoid interruptions unless it's an emergency.

You do not use time productively, before you see patients. Use the time to catch up on answering emails or replying to messages.

You stay late to finish work or take it home to do in the evenings, then you need to change.

6. Are you overwhelmed?

Your training emphasises compassion and empathy for your patients' needs. However, this can sometimes lead to difficulties in saying 'no' to patients or other demands on your time.

It is important to understand that you have limited time and resources to provide care to all patients. Saying 'no' can be challenging, but it is a necessary skill to prevent burnout and ensure that you can provide the best possible care to patients.

There are several reasons you may struggle with saying 'no.' You may feel guilty or worried about letting down your patients or may fear negative consequences such as complaints or losing patients. The pressure to meet targets can contribute to difficulties in setting boundaries. With only ten minutes allocated for each patient, every second counts.

You may glance at the clock as your first patient comes into the room. After welcoming him with a warm smile, you ask, 'What brings you here today?'

As he explains his symptoms, perhaps an annoying cough and a slight fever, you take notes, as your mind considers how to deal with the problem presented. You listen intently, nodding occasionally while trying to extract the most relevant information within the constrained timeframe.

With only minutes left, you wrap up the consultation, offering a quick physical check-up, and offering a prescription if it seems necessary and suggesting that the patient returns if the symptoms get worse.

Then you quickly move onto the next patient.

Your colleague may experience the same pressure to complete the consultation in record time.

You learn to guide the conversation by asking targeted questions to narrow down potential causes. Your years of experience enable you to identify both urgent concerns and those treatable with lifestyle adjustments.

Despite the ticking clock, you show a genuine connection, ensuring each patient feels heard and cared for, all while balancing the demands of a busy clinic.

As the ten-minute mark approaches, you jot notes, scribbling referrals and follow-up recommendations. You saw each encounter not just as an obligation but as an opportunity to affect lives positively, though briefly.

In the ten-minute consultation, the art of medicine must be refined. You must deal with complex human stories under pressure, offering both medical advice and a glimmer of hope. As you deal with each patient, you carry the weight of responsibility, knowing that quality care may need to be delivered quickly.

To overcome these challenges, use clear communication and set realistic expectations for patients and colleagues. Delegate responsibilities when possible. Seeking support from colleagues can also provide guidance and reassurance when you face difficult situations. Overall, saying 'no' can be uncomfortable, but it is an important skill that can help your well-being.

MEET THE CHALLENGES OF WORKING AS A DOCTOR

19

7. Patients increase your workload.

'Patients make an appointment and then turn up with half the family expecting me to see them too'

Symptom: Having to see several more people during a short appointment time made for one person.

Cause: People don't appreciate, or even know, what the rules are. They think you will see them and any other family members that come along at the same time for separate medical consultations.

Result: Your intentions of keeping to time go out of the window.

Managing an appointment for a patient to see you can sometimes become complicated, especially when multiple people show up for a single time slot. Here are some strategies to ensure a smoother experience and avoid such situations.

Confirm appointments: When someone makes an appointment, confirm who is being seen. Ensure everyone involved understands the appointment's purpose and necessity for attendance.

Inform participants: Tell anyone else who may wish to attend that only the patient may enter the appointment room, unless otherwise specified.

Set rules: Specify how many people can attend, limiting it to one support person. Communicate this to the person making the appointment.

Advise on necessity: Explain why it is essential for the patient to attend alone or with limited support, for comfort or confidentiality reasons.

Virtual appointments: Consider on-line options where family members can join remotely if their presence is necessary for support or discussion.

Shared document: Use digital tools to share important information or questions that others may have, reducing the need for them to attend in person.

Pre-appointment communication: Call the doctor's clinic ahead of time to convey any special needs of the patient.

Signs and reminders: Suggest that the clinic provides clear signs about attendance policies in the reception area to prevent confusion.

Transport: If transport is a concern for multiple patients arriving together, only the one patient at a time goes into the appointment.

Drop-off and pickup: Plan where people can drop off the patient and wait outside or in a nearby area.

Discuss patient privacy: Remind family and friends that medical appointments are often sensitive, and having fewer people can help maintain privacy.

Emphasise efficiency: Focus on how a streamlined appointment with fewer attendees allows for more effective communication between the healthcare provider and patient.

Post-appointment discussion: Encourage family members or friends to discuss the appointment's content later, allowing them involvement without crowding the visit.

Feedback on experience: After the visit, gather feedback on what worked well and what didn't, to improve future attendance and appointment dynamics.

MEET THE CHALLENGES OF WORKING AS A DOCTOR

By applying these suggestions, you can help a smoother consultation experience, reducing the likelihood of multiple people attending when it isn't necessary. Communicating expectations and utilising technology can enhance the effectiveness and efficiency of medical visits.

8. Unproductive meetings.

'Most meetings are a total waste of time, but I feel I have to go'

Symptom: Unproductive meetings take too much time and achieve little.

Cause: Failure of the chairperson to set an agenda that includes keeping people on time.

Result: Attendees get irritated and bored and do not contribute effectively.

You have a demanding job dealing with patients. However, others expect you to attend ineffective meetings. Meetings are a necessary part of any organisation. However, when these meetings become ineffectual, they can be a waste of time.

The first reason you have to attend unproductive meetings is because of bureaucracy in the healthcare system. There is a lot of paperwork and administrative work involved. People often hold meetings to discuss policies, procedures, and updates. Unfortunately, these meetings can be too lengthy and drawn out.

The second reason is because of a lack of clear communication between management and healthcare professionals. While meetings may seem necessary to discuss important topics, the lack of clear agendas and the absence of effective meeting procedures can lead to ineffective discussions. When you have attended a meeting that was a waste of time, it can lead to frustration.

The third reason that you attend unproductive meetings is because of a lack of respect for your time. You must work long hours, often without breaks. Unnecessary meetings show a disregard for your time. This can precede a lack of trust between doctors and management, leading to larger issues in the future.

Improving unproductive meetings can transform them into valuable sessions that contribute to the achievement of goals and foster collaboration. Here are some steps to enhance the effectiveness of meetings:

Set clear objectives: Before arranging a meeting, explain its purpose. What does the organiser aim to achieve? It should be specific and actionable.

Distribute agenda: Send out an agenda ahead of time, outlining the topics to be discussed, and the desired outcomes.

Invite the right people: Only invite those who are essential to the discussion or can contribute significantly to the topics.

Consider roles: Ensure that participants understand their roles in the meeting to keep conversations focused and productive.

Establish ground rules: Set guidelines for participation, including how to engage in discussions respectfully and constructively.

Time management: Allocate specific time slots for each agenda item to keep the meeting on track.

Use technology wisely: Utilise tools like video conferencing, shared documents, or project management software to improve participation.

Real-time note taking: Keep track with notes during the meeting, allowing everyone to access them later.

Encourage participation: Create an environment where everyone feels comfortable sharing their ideas. Use strategies like round-robin or open forums.

Facilitate discussions: Appoint someone to guide the conversation and ensure everyone takes part.

Document decisions: Clearly record key decisions, discussions, and allotted tasks during the meeting.

Set deadlines: Assign deadlines for actions to hold participants accountable and keep momentum.

Distribute minutes: Share the meeting notes and actions promptly with all participants, even those who couldn't attend.

Review progress: Schedule follow-ups to review the status of assigned tasks in subsequent meetings or check-ins.

Assess meeting effectiveness: After the meeting, ask participants for feedback on the meeting's successes and areas for improvement.

Adapt and adjust: Use feedback to refine future meetings, ensuring they remain relevant and productive.

Evaluate the need for meetings: Consider whether a meeting is necessary, or if you can share updates using email, chat, or other less formal communication.

Regular reviews: Periodically review the meeting schedule to eliminate redundant or ineffective meetings.

By applying these strategies, you can revitalise meetings, making them more productive and engaging for all participants. Remember, the goal is to create an environment that encourages collaboration while achieving the intended outcomes efficiently.

In conclusion, you must attend meetings for a range of reasons. It is essential for healthcare organisations to take the steps to ensure that meetings are productive and efficient, providing you with the opportunity to focus on the wellbeing and care of your patients.

9. Not enough time to see patients.

Your aim is providing high-quality care to your patients. However, the amount of paperwork and/or computer input associated with being a doctor can be overwhelming and time-consuming, leaving you with less time to devote to your patients.

Maintaining accurate records and completing all necessary paperwork is essential, but it can often feel like an endless stream of forms and administrative tasks.

On top of this, you may struggle to keep up with the demands of your patients while trying to manage the admin work. Patients expect prompt responses and thorough explanations, which can be difficult to provide while also dealing with the administrative side of your practice.

The admin work associated with being a doctor is a necessary evil, but it doesn't have to affect your ability to provide high-quality care. Outsourcing certain administrative tasks, automating processes and delegating tasks to others can all help to reduce the burden of computer work on your practice.

The demand for medical attention is on the rise, and you may struggle to keep up. As the number of patients you see each day continues to increase, it has become increasingly difficult for you to find the time to provide each person with the care and attention they deserve.

With the growing population and increased life expectancy, more and more people need medical attention. This has put a great deal of strain on the healthcare system, leaving you feeling overwhelmed and overworked.

As you try to cope with the rising patient numbers, you deal with a multitude of challenges. Long work hours, insufficient staffing, and the need to keep up with the latest medical advancements all make it difficult to provide the best possible care for every patient.

The COVID-19 pandemic has added another layer of difficulty to this situation. As you focus on treating those infected with the virus, you must also continue to see your regular patients, further stretching the resources.

One of your most pressing issues is the lack of time to give patients adequate attention. The complexities of modern medicine, combined with an ever-increasing patient load, have led to situations where you struggle to deliver the quality of care that patients deserve.

The impact of time limitations. You often juggle multiple appointments throughout the day, forcing you to meet tight schedules. As a result, consultations can feel rushed, leaving both you and patients with a sense of incompleteness. Important aspects of care, such as thorough history-taking, empathetic communication, and patient education, can fall by the wayside. This not only affects the patient's experience but can also lead to misdiagnoses or overlooked symptoms.

Consequences for patient outcomes. When time is scarce, compromised care may affect long-term health outcomes. Patients may leave without a comprehensive understanding of their conditions, contributing to poor adherence to treatment plans or follow-up recommendations. In chronic disease management, where ongoing support and changing care plans are crucial, this lack of time aggravates situations and causes preventable emergencies.

The need for a systemic change. Addressing this issue requires wide-ranging changes in healthcare delivery. Solutions may include restructuring appointment schedules, integrating technology to streamline processes, and increasing the healthcare workforce to ensure that providers can spend the time with each patient. It's essential for healthcare systems to recognise that investing in adequate time for patient care not only improves patient satisfaction but also enhances overall health outcomes.

Ultimately, the challenge of insufficient time to see patients is not just a personal dilemma for you. it's a critical issue that warrants attention and action. By encouraging changes that prioritise ample time for patient interactions, a more effective and compassionate healthcare system will be possible, eventually.

10. Not planning 'catch up times.'

'I run over the allotted time and then never catch up'

Symptom: Increasingly keeping patients waiting for a long time beyond their designated appointment.

Cause: Not allowing catch-up times.

Result: Added stress and poor concentration.

You have the important task of keeping your patients healthy and providing them with the best possible care. However, one issue many patients encounter is not being able to make an appointment with their doctor.

Unfortunately, doctors rarely plan catch-up times to accommodate patients who need to reschedule or missed their appointments. This is because doctors have a tight schedule, and they must see all their patients within a certain timeframe.

Planning for 'catch-up times ensures that you have adequate time to catch up on administrative tasks, patient follow-ups, and continuing education without spoiling patient care.

Dedicated 'catch up' sessions. Set aside specific time slots each week in your calendar that are free of patient appointments.

Suggested times:

Friday afternoons

Monday mornings

Midweek slots such as Wednesday afternoons.

Duration of 'catch-up' times. Each session could last at least 2-3 hours, allowing enough time for various tasks.

Consider a longer session (4-6 hours) once a month for more extensive projects or training.

Task priorities by creating a list of tasks to prioritise during catch-up time, including:

Reviewing patient notes.

Completing documentation.

Following up on test results.

Engaging in professional development or continuing education. Responding to emails and messages.

Team coordination. Communicate with the healthcare team to ensure coverage during catch-up times. Consider rotating catch-up sessions among team members to avoid disturbance.

Utilising technology. Use tools such as electronic reminders for follow-ups.

Use scheduling software that allows for easy management of catch-up time and prevents overbooking.

Feedback loop. Establish a system to assess the effectiveness of catch-up times by providing feedback on what works and what doesn't. Adjust the schedule and approach as necessary based on feedback.

Self-care and balance. Encourage healthcare providers to use 'catch up' time not just for work-related duties but also for preventing burnout, such as taking breaks, exercising, or reviewing literature.

Develop a calendar template. Set up a weekly template that includes the designated catch-up times.

Communicate with staff. Inform all staff about the new policy and ensure everyone understands the purpose of dedicated catch-up times.

Monitor and adjust. Evaluate the plan after three months, assessing productivity and staff satisfaction. Adjust times and tasks as necessary.

Applying a structured 'catch up' time plan will help you manage your workload more effectively, ultimately leading to improved patient care and your well-being.

11. Mistake 1: Not being time aware.

When you aren't time-aware during consultations, you let the patient talk as long as they want and then you discuss at length and allow plenty of questions.

All the while, the clock is ticking and there are more patients in the waiting room getting annoyed because they came on time and you are over-running as usual, so you get stressed and they get angry. Not a good basis for a consultation, is it?

Become more time-aware. That means you will get through the patients during the designated time and get the work done so that you can leave at a reasonable time, get home and enjoy your time away.

When you cannot be time-aware during consultations, you cause frustration and inconvenience to yourself and to patients.

One of the principal ways that you cannot be time-aware is by being late for appointments. Patients may have to wait for an extended period before being seen by you which can interrupt their daily routine and cause them to be late for other commitments.

Another way that you cannot be time-aware is by spending too long with patients. While it's important to provide the best level of care, you need to balance this with the needs of other patients who are waiting to see you. Spending too long with one patient can cause a domino effect with appointments for the rest of the day.

Finally, you cannot be time-aware by overbooking appointments or not allowing time between appointments. This can lead to patients feeling rushed or unheard during their consultations and can immensely pressure you as you cannot see people on time.

You can provide the best possible care while also being respectful of your patients' time.

What can you do to become more time-aware during consultations?

Have a clock you can see easily when you look at the patient so that you are aware of time passing.

Also, have a clock that the patient can see, on your desk: so, they can also know how much time they have.

Put notices in the waiting room to educate patients about the time allotted for them: so, the patient is aware of the limitations of the consultation.

Be clear that a separate appointment is required for each person attending, to avoid multiple consultations in one time slot: to prevent several family members arriving together, all expecting you to deal with their separate problems in the space of ten minutes.

When you see it is nearly time to end the consultation, use closing techniques to show this so that you are effective at ending the consultation.

Here are some tips on how doctors can be time-aware during consultations:

- Set a realistic appointment time and try to keep it consistent. This will help you plan your day and avoid delays.
- Ask patients about their primary concerns at the beginning of the consultation. This way, you can address the most important issues first without getting side-tracked by less critical information.
- Listen carefully to your patients and take time to understand.

If you focus, you can reduce the time you spend asking questions to clarify their concerns.

- Assess and address your patient's medical issues.
- Stay organised and avoid multitasking during consultations. Multitasking can reduce the quality of care you provide to your patients.
- Use technology to improve your efficiency. For example, electronic medical records and digital medical devices can save time and provide a more accurate diagnosis.
- Plan your day, including breaks, so that you can make the most of your time. Remember to prioritise your patients' needs while also respecting your own time and well-being.

More ways to be time aware.

Time management in medical consultations is crucial for providing quality care while ensuring that patients feel heard and valued. Here are several strategies you can employ to become more time-aware during your consultations:

Set clear objectives for each consultation: Prior to each appointment, outline key objectives you want to achieve. This helps streamline the conversation and keeps the focus on essential topics.

Utilise time limits: Allocate specific time slots for different parts of the consultation (e.g., history taking, examination, discussion). Use a timer or watch discreetly to stay on track without being disruptive.

Implement structure: Use standardised templates for common conditions or visits. This saves time and ensures you cover all necessary information efficiently.

Practice active listening: Focus on truly listening to the patient to avoid misunderstandings that can lead to repeated questions or extended explanations. This can help in quickly identifying the main issues.

Prioritise questions: Encourage patients to share their most pressing concerns first. This helps address the most important issues within the allocated time.

Educate patients on time management: Inform patients about the time constraints at the beginning of the consultation. Encourage them to come prepared with questions or to focus on their top concerns.

Streamline documentation: Use electronic medical records effectively by employing templates or shortcuts for documentation. Consider voice recognition tools to save time during notetaking.

Delegate appropriately: Empower other healthcare staff to handle tasks that do not require your expertise, such as collecting preliminary information or follow-up scheduling, allowing the you to concentrate on assessment and care.

Reflect on consultations: After each consultation, reflect on what went well and what you could improve regarding time management. This self-assessment can lead to more effective practices.

Stay flexible: While it's important to adhere to time frames, be prepared to adjust if a patient presents complex issues that require more attention. Prioritising patient care over strict timelines is essential, but balance is key.

Use technology wisely: Implement telemedicine or digital health tools that can facilitate quicker follow-up consultations for minor issues, freeing up time for more complex cases.

By integrating these strategies into your practice, you can enhance their time awareness during consultations, ultimately leading to improved patient satisfaction and outcomes. Balancing efficiency with compassionate care is vital.

By using these tips, you can be more time aware during consultations, providing the best possible care to your patients.

12. Mistake 2: Solving problems too quickly.

Your patient has a ten-minute slot, and you want to do your best for them. They tell you several symptoms and you listen and nod empathically. Then they tell you about how they have lost their job and don't know how they will afford the rent next month. You try to stay focused but you glance at the clock and realise the 10 minutes are almost over and you don't have a clue what to address first. This patient has so many issues to deal with, they need about four appointments to sort them all out.

So, you start one by one while being aware of the building numbers in the waiting room and the ticking clock.

Educate the patients about the time allowance for each consultation so that they realise they have to get to the point.

Ask them to be specific about what they want from you today (rather than 'tell me all your problems about anything'): so that they tell you what they want, specifically from this consultation.

If it seems like too much to deal with in the short allotted time, ask them to book a double appointment for the next consultation: then you can give them longer attention.

Ask them what they are really worried about or what they think causes their symptoms so that you can address this.

Your workload is heavy, and your time is valuable. However, stop trying to solve all of your patients' problems in just ten minutes.

Medical problems are often complex and require a comprehensive approach to diagnosis and treatment. Rushing through a consultation can lead to misdiagnosis or overlooking important symptoms.

This approach often neglects the emotional and psychological needs of patients. Medical problems can be scary and overwhelming, and patients need reassurance and support. By rushing through appointments, you risk leaving your patients feeling unheard and uncared for.

There is pressure to see as many patients as possible in a day, but prioritise quality over quantity. Patients rely on your expertise to guide them to better health, and that takes time and attention.

How can you deal with a patient with multiple problems?

Dealing with a patient who presents multiple medical issues requires a comprehensive and systematic approach. Here are some strategies you can implement for the effective management of such cases.

Comprehensive history taking: Gather detailed information about the patient's medical history, current symptoms, and any medications they are taking.

Physical examination: Conduct a thorough physical examination to evaluate all reported issues.

Diagnostic tests: Order relevant tests to gather more information and identify any underlying conditions.

Identify the most urgent problems: Assess which conditions pose the greatest risk or require immediate intervention. Addressing life-threatening issues first is crucial.

Sorting: Group problems into categories (e.g., acute vs. chronic, psychological vs. physical) to streamline the treatment process.

MEET THE CHALLENGES OF WORKING AS A DOCTOR

Develop a treatment plan: Engage in shared decision-making with the patient to prioritise treatment goals and preferences.

Integrated approach: Create a multilayered treatment plan that addresses multiple issues simultaneously, when possible, rather than treating each problem in isolation.

Follow evidence-based guidelines: Utilise clinical guidelines for managing co-morbidities for a more structured approach.

Referrals to specialists: Consider involving specialists for complex issues that require specific expertise.

Team-based care: Co-operate with a healthcare team: including nurses, therapists, social workers, and pharmacists, to provide holistic care that addresses physical, emotional, and social aspects.

Empower the patient: Educate the patient about their conditions, treatment options, and lifestyle changes that may improve their overall health.

Support systems: Encourage the use of support groups or counselling services to address mental health or social challenges associated with their multiple health issues.

Monitor Progress: Arrange regular follow-up appointments to assess the effectiveness of the treatment plan, make necessary adjustments, and maintain open lines of communication.

Flexibility: Be prepared to change the treatment plan as the patient's condition develops or fresh problems arise.

Address psychosocial factors: Understand how psychological and social factors may affect the patient's health and integrate mental health support into their care.

Lifestyle and well-being: Encourage healthy lifestyle choices (diet, exercise, stress management) to positively affect multiple conditions.

Keep accurate records: Ensure thorough records of the patient's medical history, treatment plans, and progress notes. This helps continuity of care.

Coordinate with primary care providers: Maintain communication with the patient's primary care physician and other healthcare providers involved in their care.

By employing these strategies, you can effectively manage patients with multiple problems, leading to improved health outcomes and enhanced patient satisfaction. Slow down and take the time necessary to properly diagnose and treat your patients. It may take a little longer, but the payoff for both you and your patients will be significant.

MEET THE CHALLENGES OF WORKING AS A DOCTOR

47

13. Mistake 3: Not using morning time.

You arrive at your workplace with about half an hour before seeing patients. Maybe you have a cup of coffee or chat with your colleagues or check your emails. A bit of this and a bit of that until it's time to see the first patient.

It doesn't seem worth starting any of the bigger jobs you have to do. You always do those when you come in to catch up on a Saturday or Sunday morning.

However, instead of using that slot of time unstructured, you could use it to:

Open your letters so that you are ready to answer and deal with them.

- Read through any results so that you are prepared to tell the patient what to do next.
- Check and sign any typed letters to get that task done and out of the way.
- Plan what you will do for the rest of the day in order to prioritise your workload.
- Look at and answer your emails: so that your inbox is clear before you start work.

Your time is valuable. Your patients rely on you for their medical care, and every minute of your time is important to them. Therefore, it's essential that you use your time effectively before seeing patients.

Here are a few tips to better use your time:

Before your patients arrive, make sure you have all the information on hand. Review their medical records, lab results, and any other relevant data that may be pertinent to their visit. This will help you stay ahead of the game and ensure you can provide the best care possible.

- Take a few minutes to make a to-do list and prioritise your tasks for the day. Focus on the most critical items first, such as reviewing test results and deciding which patients need follow-up care. This will help you manage your workload and prevent important tasks from slipping through the cracks.
- Reduce wasted time. Consider investing in technology to automate certain aspects of your work. This will help you be more efficient and make the most of your time.
- Look after yourself by eating a healthy breakfast, staying hydrated, and taking a few deep breaths before your first patient.

By using your time effectively before seeing patients, you can provide better care, manage your workload more efficiently, and prevent burnout. Take the time to prepare, streamline, and care for yourself.

14. Mistake 4: Allowing interruptions.

You are getting through your clinic list and seeing each patient at his or her designated time.

But you congratulate yourself too soon! There is a knock at the door and the receptionist wants to tell you a complicated story she has just heard from a patient on the phone. You say you'll take the call and listen again to the multiple symptoms from one of your regular heart-sink patients.

You listen and finally suggest she make an appointment to see you. A glance at the clock and you realise this has taken twenty minutes, so you are now running late. You feel your stress level has risen, as you call in the next patient.

There is another way: Make a strict rule about no interruptions while seeing patients, or during your designated admin time, unless there is an emergency.

Designate a time each day when you are not seeing patients and will accept calls from patients and staff. If there are no queries during that time, use it to catch up on routine tasks.

You are a crucial part of the healthcare system. You diagnose and treat patients effectively. You need to have extensive knowledge, excellent multitasking abilities, and be able to keep track of many tasks simultaneously. Therefore, you require an interruption-free environment.

However, if you are continually being interrupted, your ability to focus on patient care is affected. Patients, colleagues, administrative staff, and other healthcare professionals are among the many people who create distractions. Interruptions can cause medical errors and misdiagnoses.

One of the worst disruptions is when you are interrupted during patient consultations or procedures. Consultations are essential and you must focus on the patient's condition. Therefore, concentrate single-mindedly on a task to avoid any disturbances or interruptions.

To prevent interruptions, close the door while in consultation with a patient. This allows you to provide better patient care.

Another distraction is the administrative work you must do, whether it's completing documentation, filling forms, or responding to emails. Time-management is extremely crucial and a lack of control over your time can be frustrating. To combat this, you need administrative support to help manage these tasks, freeing up time to concentrate on your patient's needs.

15. Mistake 5: Not delegating enough.

Delegating is fine in theory, but sometimes you do jobs that are not supposed to be your responsibility. It's easy to feel sympathy for other overworked team members. However, you won't be helping anyone in the long term if you do someone else's job instead of addressing what needs to be done to change the system.

What do you do if the practice nurse refuses to take the bloods and you end up taking them all?

Ask yourself:

- Whose job is it?
- Are you covering up the failures of the system?
- How do other practices manage?
- Are you ordering too many tests?

One practice might solve the problem by employing someone specifically to take blood. Another asks patients to come back the next day or at another time for an appointment specifically for blood to be taken.

You can introduce another system. It takes about three weeks for it to become automatic. Think of the time you spend doing things that don't need your qualifications and decide to put new boundaries in place.

What difference would this make in your life?

You prefer to do something rather than ask someone else. You don't want to explain to them what to do and then check up on them afterwards.

But you don't have enough hours in the day to do everything yourself.

There is another way:

Make a note during the day of the non-specialist tasks you do.

- Decide whom you could ask to do them for you.
- Don't expect them to read your mind.
- Tell them exactly what you want them to do.
- Train them
- Trust them.
- Praise them for what they do right.
- Explain what you want done differently.

To provide better care for your patients, it is vital that you learn to delegate tasks to free up your time and reduce your workload.

How can you delegate effectively?

Delegation is an essential skill for you, allowing you to improve your work, increase patient care, and reduce stress. Effective delegation can lead to greater teamwork, better resource management, and increased job satisfaction.

Here are several strategies to help you delegate effectively:

Understand your strengths and limitations: Begin by assessing your own skills and workload. Identifying tasks that are time-consuming or outside your expertise can help you decide what to delegate.

Know your team: Understand the strengths, weaknesses, and expertise of your team members, including nurses, physician assistants, and administrative staff. This knowledge enables you to assign tasks to the right individuals who can handle them effectively.

Establish clear goals and expectations: When delegating a task, ensure that the objectives are clear. Outline the expected outcomes, timelines, and any specific procedures that need to be followed. This clarity helps prevent misunderstandings and miscommunication.

Provide adequate training and resources: Ensure that team members have the training and tools to perform delegated tasks effectively. Providing resources, support, and guidance can enhance their confidence and competence.

Encourage open communication: Support an environment where team members feel comfortable asking questions and providing feedback. Open communication helps identify potential issues early and ensures that everyone agrees.

Trust your team: Once you have delegated a task, trust your colleagues to carry it out. Micromanaging can undermine their confidence and lead to frustrations. Give them the autonomy to complete the task while remaining available for support as needed.

Monitor progress: Check in regularly to monitor progress without hovering. This allows you to stay informed and address any challenges that arise while still allowing team members to take ownership of their responsibilities.

Be flexible: Be willing to adjust tasks or responsibilities as necessary based on changing circumstances or feedback from your team. Flexibility can lead to more efficient workflows and better outcomes.

Offer recognition and feedback: Acknowledge the efforts and accomplishments of your team. Providing constructive feedback and recognising their contributions fosters a positive work environment and encourages continued growth and development.

Evaluate and reflect: After delegating, take time to evaluate the outcomes and the process. Determine what worked well and what could improve future delegations. Continuous improvement will strengthen your delegation skills.

By implementing these strategies, you can delegate effectively, enabling you to focus on high-level clinical tasks while allowing your team members to contribute significantly to patient care.

Effective delegation not only enhances efficiency, but also encourages a collaborative and supportive workplace. Delegation allows you to focus on your core responsibilities, - patient care, while other professionals handle extra tasks. By delegating these tasks, you can get more done, which ultimately leads to better patient outcomes.

Delegation is not a sign of weakness, but a clever strategy to reduce stress. By delegating, you can also reduce the risk of making errors or lapses in judgement because of fatigue or stress.

MEET THE CHALLENGES OF WORKING AS A DOCTOR

16. Mistake 6: Not streamlining tasks.

You have several routine tasks you do each day. If you are taking longer than necessary to do these, then you would benefit from devising a much more efficient strategy for getting things done.

Spending too long on simple tasks delays everything else. Usually, you can speed up tasks by making simple changes. When you do things as efficiently as possible, then you do them more quickly and so free up more time to finish earlier. Notice what your daily tasks are and be creative in your thinking about them.

In the healthcare environment, you face the challenge of managing your time and resources efficiently while delivering high-quality patient care.

Streamline your tasks by:

- Having equipment to use on the patient close to hand so that when you need to take blood pressure or listen to a chest, you don't have to move across the room to get your sphygmomanometer or stethoscope.
- Making sure you can input into the computer and talk to the patient with as little as possible shift in your chair.
- Making a chart to list routine tasks for yourself.
- Deciding a time of day for admin tasks.
- Creating a to-do list in order of importance to manage tasks efficiently. Prioritising tasks is essential, especially when dealing with emergencies or critical situations.
- Creating a daily and weekly plan for your tasks that can help you allocate your time efficiently. Breaking down your day into blocks of time ensures that you can tackle your tasks in manageable chunks.

- Using technology: Utilise electronic tools like calendars, reminder apps, and scheduling software to keep a record of your tasks. Fully using electronic systems can reduce paperwork and enable quicker access to patient information. Streamlined documentation processes, such as voice recognition for charting, can also save time.
- Delegating non-essential or non-medical tasks to other members of your team can free up valuable time for you to focus on patient care. It can include administrative tasks, booking appointments, or managing paperwork.
- Minimising interruptions: When possible, close your door, turn off your phone, and close your email. These measures can help you tackle tasks without interruption and improve overall productivity.
- Developing checklists for routine procedures and treatments to save time and reduce mistakes.
- Offering virtual consultations can help manage patient loads more effectively, allowing for more flexible scheduling and reducing the time spent on non-critical in-person visits.
- Using scheduling software can help improve appointment slots while minimising waiting times. Blocking specific times for certain types of visits (e.g., follow-ups, new patients) can help maintain a balanced schedule.
- Double-booking for routine visits: In certain scenarios, double-booking patients for routine, shorter visits can optimise time, provided it's carefully avoided excessive delays.
- Using support staff: Nurses, physician assistants, and administrative staff can take on routine tasks, allowing you to focus on more complex patient care. Training staff to handle specific procedures or tasks can also enhance efficiency.
- By delegating tasks such as prescription refills or basic patient education to trained personnel, you can save valuable time.

- Developing and adhering to evidence-based procedures can help standardise care and decrease decision-making time. This can streamline processes for common conditions, leading to faster treatment times.
- Digital reminders for routine tasks, such as patient follow-up and lab tests, help avoid missing steps.
- Holding regular team meetings to discuss challenges and facilitate improvements collaboratively.
- Encourage patients to use online portals for scheduling appointments, accessing test results, and communicating with healthcare teams can reduce phone traffic and streamline administrative tasks.
- Sending out questionnaires to patients before their visits can gather necessary information in advance, allowing for more focused consultations.
- Implement stress management techniques and ensure you have adequate time off can prevent burnout. This enables you to work more efficiently when you are on duty.

You can create a more streamlined work practice that leads to improved patient satisfaction and care outcomes.

17. Mistake 7: Not completing minor tasks.

Multiple tasks that require your attention simultaneously can overwhelm you. This is stressful and lead to burnout. One way to combat this is by completing tasks in small steps.

You don't get things done because you don't have several hours or all day to spend doing them. You say you'll get that done 'when I have time,' somehow or other, 'time' of that size doesn't seem to happen.

Suddenly, the task is both urgent and important. Complete your tax return by tomorrow!

There is another way:

- Break down enormous tasks into small pieces. Designate time every day to do part of the task.
- Set a timer for half an hour and see how much you can get done in that time.
- Change activities every half an hour.
- Find small amounts of time by identifying time wasters.
- If the task is 'desk work', leave the paperwork in a special area of your desk so you can get back to it easily
- Determine what needs to be done urgently and what can wait. This will help you focus on the most important tasks first.
- If you have an enormous task to complete, break it down into smaller, more manageable pieces. This will make it easier to tackle and avoid overwhelming you.
- It's essential to take breaks in between tasks to refresh your mind and avoid burnout. Use this time to stretch, meditate, or do something enjoyable.
- Celebrating minor achievements can help you stay motivated

and energised, even when the overall task is daunting.

Breaking down tasks into smaller chunks can make daunting projects more manageable and enhance productivity. Here's a guide to effectively breaking down tasks step by step.

Step 1: Identify the main task

Start by clearly defining the principal task you want to accomplish. Ensure you have a solid understanding of the end goal.

Step 2: Define other steps

Think about all the components necessary to complete the main task. Write everything that comes to mind, regardless of how small or trivial it may seem.

Step 3: Categorise and organise

Group similar subtasks together. This helps you see the different aspects of the primary task and can provide a clearer path forward. You might categorise them by type, phase, or dependency.

Step 4: Prioritise

Decide the order in which to complete the subtasks. Some tasks may need to be done before others, while others may be more critical to the project's success.

Step 5: Define timeframes and deadlines

Estimate how long each subtask will take. Set realistic deadlines to keep yourself on track. Consider breaking down each subtask further if necessary.

Step 6: Create a checklist or to-do list

Turn your subtasks into a checklist. Keeping track of completed tasks can provide a sense of achievement and keep you motivated.

Step 7: Review and adjust

Regularly review your progress and adjust your plans as necessary. If you find certain subtasks are taking longer than expected, reassess and change deadlines.

Step 8: Stay flexible

While it's essential to have a plan, being adaptable will help you handle unforeseen challenges effectively. Adjust your approach based on what works best as you progress.

By following these steps, you can turn an overwhelming task into a series of manageable steps, making it easier to stay focused and productive.

You'll achieve more, feel less overwhelmed, and maintain your well-being.

18. Doctors neglect their well-being.

Health and well-being results from looking after your body, mind and spirit, by eating healthily, taking regular exercise and being aware of a world beyond that of work and patients, by connecting with nature, meditation, or with more formal religious practice.

It does not mean expecting to be fit and well while eating junk food, avoiding exercise, having excessive alcohol, smoking or not stimulating your mind.

This is important because when you look after yourself, you can better look after your patients. When you don't care about yourself, how can you give the best care to your patients?

Your patients may perceive you or even yourself as the embodiment of strength and resilience. You are the healer who tirelessly cares for others, putting patient needs above your own. However, this may lead to the neglect of your own well-being.

The demanding hours, the life-or-death decisions, and emotional toll of caregiving can lead you to self-neglect. Although trained to look after patients, you may forget that you, too, are human with personal needs and vulnerabilities. The long shifts, the constant pressure, and the emotional weight of handling critical situations can take a severe toll on your mental and physical health.

Burnout has become alarmingly common among healthcare professionals. According to recent studies, a significant percentage of doctors experience symptoms of burnout, including exhaustion, cynicism, and reduced professional efficacy. The fear that admitting struggles is a weakness in such a demanding profession worsens this problem.

The culture of medicine often perpetuates the idea that self-sacrifice is synonymous with dedication. You may feel that taking time off for personal health or even arranging a day for self-care is unprofessional or selfish.

Poor mental or physical health can diminish the quality of patient care. The irony is that the very individuals tasked with caring for others are often the ones in need of care themselves.

Encouraging open dialogues about well-being and creating an environment where you feel safe to express struggles can help shift the culture away from self-neglect.

How can you improve your health and well-being straight away?

Start by taking a walk each day, eating regular meals, avoiding unhealthy food and connecting with nature.

You spend your time looking after the health and well-being of other people. It's easy to forget that your own health is just as important. It's essential to take care of your physical, mental, and emotional needs to avoid burnout and provide the best possible care for your patients.

Here are some tips on how to improve your health and well-being:

Getting sufficient sleep. If you work work long hours you may neglect their sleep. However, getting enough sleep is crucial for your mental and physical health. Aim for at least seven hours of sleep each night and try to stick to a regular sleep schedule.

Eating healthy, nutritious food is essential for your physical health. Fuel your body with plenty of fruits, vegetables, whole grains, lean proteins, and healthy fats.

MEET THE CHALLENGES OF WORKING AS A DOCTOR

Drinking enough water throughout the day is crucial for your health. Keep a water bottle with you and aim to drink at least eight glasses of water each day.

Regular exercise not only boosts your physical health but also improves your mental health. Aim to exercise for at least 30 minutes each day, even if it's just a brisk walk.

Taking breaks throughout your workday can help prevent burnout and improve your productivity. Take brief breaks every hour to stretch, go for a quick walk, or simply clear your mind.

Making time for activities that make you happy and help you relax. You could read, listen to music, practise yoga, or anything else that helps you unwind.

Don't be afraid to seek support from colleagues, friends, or mental health professionals if you're feeling stressed or overwhelmed.

19. Doctors neglect friends and families.

Finding time for friends and family means keeping a connection with people other than yourself and your patients.

It means making time to talk to friends and family on the telephone, Zoom, FaceTime, WhatsApp or face-to-face. Share what you've been doing this week, reminisce, and make each other laugh.

Keeping in touch with others away from work helps you relax and appreciate that there is a life outside of Medicine.

Stop being vague about meeting friends 'sometime or other' when 'we are not so busy,' and instead decide a time for socialising in your diary so that it is as important as your work commitments.

It's challenging to find time for the people outside of work. Medical professionals work long hours, are on call, and have extremely busy schedules. However, it's important to make time for friends and family to maintain a healthy work-life balance. Here are some tips to help you find time for your loved ones.

One of the best ways to make time for friends and family is by arranging activities in advance. Whether it's a weekly dinner or a monthly outing, making plans ensures that you have something to look forward to and can work your diary around it.

It's crucial to be efficient with your time. Try to set up meetings or appointments near your home or near the activities you'll be doing with your friends and family. This will allow you to commute less and more time, enjoying your loved ones' company.

t's essential to set aside time each day to recharge your batteries. Whether it's exercising, meditating, or reading, taking time for yourself will allow you to clear your mind and have a more balanced timetable.

You have a team of health-care colleagues working with you. Delegating responsibilities can help ease your workload and free up time for leisure activities. Delegating tasks to others can also help build their skills and confidence.

When you find the time for friends and family, make sure you're mentally present. Put away your phone and any work-related materials and focus on the people you're spending time with. Being present and fully engaged in the moment will help strengthen your relationships and create lasting memories.

Finding time for friends and family can be challenging, but it's crucial to maintain a healthy work-life balance. With a little planning, you can create a space in your busy life for the people you love. Remember to be present in the moment and enjoy the time you have with your loved ones.

MEET THE CHALLENGES OF WORKING AS A DOCTOR

20. Doctors must take time out.

How often do you take 'time out' for your own relaxation and re-charging your 'personal battery?'.

Everyone needs time for rest and relaxation, including you, especially if you work excessively long hours and by the time you finish each day, all you can do is eat and sleep.

When you take 'time out', you discover that you have more energy for the work you must do and will do it more efficiently and effectively than when you are exhausted and burnt out.

Take a few minutes between patients to be aware of your breath. Breathe in and out slowly, five times, noticing your breath going in through your nose as you tell yourself that you are breathing in relaxation and breathing out tension and stress.

Then learn about being more mindful by taking brief breaks during the day when you either sit and appreciate your life and surroundings or go for a short walk and really notice the details of where you are.

Eventually, you will take 'time out' regularly and include designated time for things other than seeing patients and the connected work involved, and be able to enjoy life in a more relaxed way.

Your life can be hectic and stressful. You are constantly dealing with patients and their families, making critical decisions, and meeting deadlines. Finding time to relax and recharge your batteries can seem like an impossible task. However, taking a break for your personal well-being is necessary to provide the best care for your patients.

Here are some tips on how to take time out for yourself to relax and recharge:

Make it a priority to plan time for activities that recharge you. It could be anything from reading a book, taking a walk, or practicing yoga to something as simple as sipping your favourite drink or taking a nap.

When you aren't working, make sure you disconnect from work altogether. Try not to check your emails or take work calls, if you are not on call. Separating work from personal time helps you relax and switch off from the constant pressure of work.

Taking a holiday is the easiest way to recharge your batteries. It provides a change of scenery and allows you to unwind completely. Plan a holiday that involves activities you enjoy or plan to take part in activities that are completely new to you.

Having a hobby is a great way to take your mind off work and focus on something that you enjoy. It can be anything from playing a musical instrument, gardening, or painting.

Exercise helps reduce stress and provides the perfect way to move your body and feel energised. Make it a habit to exercise regularly to maintain a healthy body and mind.

Taking time out for yourself is crucial for your mental and physical well-being. Planning time for personal activities, disconnecting from work, taking a holiday, finding a hobby, and exercising regularly are easy ways to recharge your batteries. Make it a practice to take care of yourself and your well-being, and you find it reflects in your work as well.

MEET THE CHALLENGES OF WORKING AS A DOCTOR

21. Time management for doctors.

If you say to yourself: 'the day isn't long enough to do all that...' then better time management is the way to get things done. If you want to do something that you are not doing now, then you must change - you could start with your attitude to your daily tasks.

No matter how busy you are, if wanting to do more frustrates you, you must become more aware of your time and see how you spend your day.

Do this by logging what you are doing for a couple of days. Then it will be easier to identify where to make changes because you will notice more easily what you do you could do differently.

There may be more efficient ways to organise your work. It's easy to get into the routine of doing something a particular way, but there may be a more efficient way to do it. Sometimes it helps to ask a friend or colleague for their opinion about whether there might be a quicker way to do some of your jobs.

You can devise a system to automate part, or all, of what you do. You may have to let go of your need to do everything, or the belief that only you can do a good job, and delegate more to others. Understand that others could do some of your tasks equally well.

How long is it since you thought about your daily routine, and about what you could stop doing altogether? Routines become habits that are rarely re-examined or re-assessed to check whether they still need to be done at all.

Once you've decided what to delegate and have identified and discarded time-wasters, and have been as efficient as possible with what remains, you can then enjoy yourself. If you identify what you will do with the newly created time, then you are much more likely to do it.

Decide your goals:

- Set realistic goals achievable in the time available
- Prioritising your goals in order of importance
- Setting deadlines for each goal
- Creating a plan of action for each goal
- Taking action towards each goal
- Evaluating your progress and readjusting your goals and priorities as necessary

Until you know what you want to achieve, how will you know when you've got there?

In order to manage your day more effectively, become very clear about what you want to get done during each day. Not only each day, but also what you want to achieve by the end of the week, by the end of the month, and by the end of the year.

Knowing the clinics, ward rounds, visits, and the patients who need to be seen allows you to plan your day.

Be clear about what you can do each day and still have some time and energy left for after work rest and relaxation.

When you manage your time effectively, you will become much clearer about what you're trying to achieve and organise ways you can do this more efficiently. You also find that when you plan your day, you get things done. By achieving, moving towards your goals, you will gradually feel more in control and less stressed.

You may make some of these time management mistakes. You are probably doing several things that you could easily delegate to someone else. Maybe you think it's quicker just to get it done yourself.

MEET THE CHALLENGES OF WORKING AS A DOCTOR

In the long term, it's better to teach someone what you want done, in relation to tasks which don't have to be done by you, supervise them until they can do them appropriately. This may use some of your time at first, but in the long term, this will free up more time for you.

81

22. Get organised.

If your life and your possessions are chaotic and you feel as though you never have enough time to do what you really want to do, then it's important to spend a designated amount of time getting more organised.

Make sure that your workspace is clear except for whatever you need in order to get on with the job you have set yourself. Put things away and keep similar things together so that it's easy to find them again.

Throw away papers and other things that you no longer need. Become better at "letting things go". You find that when the surrounding space becomes more organised, so does your thinking. You will do much more in a brief space of time.

Eliminate your time wasters, be more efficient in the way you do things.

Instead of using too much work as an excuse not to have a social life, make your life outside of work a vital part of your week.

Plan to spend time with your partner, friends and family and get involved in community activities.

Decide specifically what you want in these important areas of your life, and then look at the ways you can achieve what you want. Take the steps to create the time to have a rewarding professional life and also a fulfilling life outside of work.

When you do this, you will plan and think more clearly about the patient in front of you instead of worrying about what you did with other patients.

Keep focused. Break down your tasks into smaller steps to avoid distraction and achieve your goals one step at a time. Don't be distracted by other non-urgent, non-important things.

Keep your goal for the day in mind and finish one step at a time. In a clinic setting, for instance, instruct others to interrupt you only if it's a dire emergency.

The receptionist may feel his or her job is done when they tell you something. Suggest they put the information on paper for you to collect between appointments.

Vary what you do. This is a great way to keep motivated. You may find, for example, that changing the sort of task you do every hour is an effective way to get several things done during the day. This works best if you change from a desk-based activity to doing something which involves more physical activity.

Variety is the spice of life: Do different things and keep progressing with all of them, instead of spending a huge amount of time on one task only.

You may find that seeing a few patients and then handling some administrative tasks or phone calls keeps you progressing and prevents an enormous task from accumulating after patient visits.

Set time limits. As a general guideline, it is advisable to set a realistic time limit.

Acknowledge what you get done. Some people become frustrated when they feel they are not achieving very much. However, if you devise a way to make a note when you finish each step of your project, then you will be much more aware of how you are progressing. This might tick items on the list.

Take breaks and allow yourself some free time, especially when you're feeling overwhelmed or stressed. Taking a few minutes to yourself can help you regroup and refocus, so you can be more productive when you return to your work.

Say no to requests that will take up too much of your time to protect your time and energy. When you say no to something, you are saying yes to something else.

Delegate tasks you can't or don't have time to do. Then you are giving someone else the responsibility to complete a specific task. This can be an effective way to free up your own time so that you can focus on other areas of your work. It is important to select the right person for the job and to provide them with simple instructions.

Outsourcing is like delegating in that you are giving someone else the responsibility to complete a task. However, with outsourcing, you usually hire a third-party company or individual to complete the work.

Avoid procrastination. Tips to avoid procrastination include:

- Finding a specific goal to focus on
- Breaking down tasks into smaller, more manageable steps
- Setting deadlines and creating a plan of action
- Eliminating distractions
- Seeking professional help if procrastination is severely affecting your life

23. Learn to manage your stress levels.

What things in your life are causing you to feel stressed? Once you know what your stressors are, you can address them. Here are a few tips to help you:

- Find healthy ways to cope with stress. This can include exercise, meditation, journalling, or spending time with friends and family.
- Avoid unhealthy coping mechanisms, such as alcohol or drugs. These can actually make your stress levels worse in the long run.
- Make time for relaxation. Make time each day to do things you enjoy and that help you relax.
- Learn to say no. Don't take on more than you can handle. If you're feeling overwhelmed, it's okay to say no to additional commitments.

By following these tips, you can manage your stress levels and improve your overall wellbeing. Don't get frustrated. You are not getting much done. You are possibly doing more than you thought you were. If you make a list and tick the items as you do them, you will recognise your progress and feel a great sense of achievement too.

What is an important tool to help you manage your time and reduce your stress? Stephen Covey in his book 'The seven habits of highly effective people' recommends classifying each of your daily activities into one or other of four quadrants. This means deciding if what you want to do is urgent and important, urgent and not important, not urgent but important, or not urgent and not important.

When you think about your activities in relation to these quadrants, you will realise how you spend your time and in what ways you need to change. Many people spend a huge amount of time doing things that are urgent but not important. An example of these activities would be answering the phone, talking to people who interrupt your flow of work, and responding to people knocking at your door.

If something is urgent and important, then you have to attend to it. For example, if somebody collapses, then you must deal with it immediately. However, aim to do most of your tasks in the quadrant that is for things that are important and not urgent. That means that when you know that a certain piece of work has to be done with the deadline that you plan to do the work over the time available rather than trying to do it all the day before, it's due. Because the more you plan what you're going to do every day means that you gradually get your tasks completed and that results in you feeling much less stressed.

Examine carefully and think about the things you do which are neither urgent nor important and eliminate as many of these as possible. Of course, these may include activities you need for your rest and relaxation or they may be purely be time wasters such as watching too much television.

If you have children to take to school before you arrive at work, make sure you get their things ready for school before you go to bed.

It's vital to have enough sleep. That may mean going to bed earlier.

Set your alarm early enough to wake up and get yourself ready without panic or rush.

Always eat breakfast. Skipping breakfast and surviving on coffee leads to a drop in blood sugar mid-morning, eating too much sugary food and to unhealthy eating later in the day

Too many time-wasters. Notice, by logging your activities as you go through your day, if you are doing some things that you could stop doing altogether. These may be tasks you could do more efficiently or things you do just because you were told years ago that your predecessor used to do this or that.

Notice how much time you spend chatting over a coffee.

Observe your most stressed colleagues and how they get through their day.

- They never take a break for lunch because they haven't time to get through the patients, anyway.
- They take work home with them because there is so much to do they can't get it done during the day.
- They never go out with friends. They have very few of them because they are always too busy to accept any social invitation, so no-one asks them anymore.
- They invite no one to meet them after work because the concept of 'after work' is foreign to them.
- They rarely smile or laugh because they take their job so seriously. Life is too serious to laugh, isn't it? You can't get on with the jobs at hand when you make fun of a situation.
- They rarely take a holiday because they have too much to do and what would you do on holiday, anyway? They occasionally make an exception and attend medical conferences.
- They don't know what relaxation means because they think that if they stop, they might never start again.
- They only read medical books and journals; the thought of reading a novel horrifies them, because they believe they must spend every spare minute staying current, reading the latest journals and catching all important medical news.

Instead, they could choose to:

- keep to designated time when seeing patients
- take a break for lunch
- stop taking work home
- meet friends
- have a laugh and don't take life so seriously
- have a regular holiday
- take a few moments every day to relax
- read a novel

Notice how life changes for the better when you change your habits in this way.

You can have more energy, feel happier, get through the workload more quickly and enjoy life much more.

24. Improve your self-care.

When you care for yourself, you will inevitably be in a better state to care for others more effectively.

It is a common mistake that people in the caring professions, such as doctors, forget how important it is to look after themselves. Perfectionism may cause them to prioritise others' care over their own. This means that they never find the time to do things for themselves.

Does this apply to you?

If you feel guilty when you say to yourself, "I am going home now," and try to keep going while there is a demand on your services, however late that may make the ending of your day, then it's important to make some changes.

However many hours you work, and how much you do, there always comes a point at which you must stop. This may be because you've finished all the tasks that need to be done, or you feel so exhausted that you cannot do one more thing. Unfortunately, if you don't stop until an illness affects you and means you must take time away from work.

Only then you will realise you are not indispensable and that it is important to work efficiently but have time away from Medicine too.

When you cannot look after yourself and cannot decide when it's time to stop, then you may find that the quality of your work deteriorates because you take longer to do routine tasks and become more likely to make mistakes.

When you make mistakes, that's when you may become a liability. Doctors who don't look after themselves may prescribe the wrong treatment or the wrong dose with subsequent serious effects both for the patient and the doctor him or herself.

Make a promise to yourself that you will look after your own needs more than you have in the past. Decide what you are going to do that will contribute to this. Perhaps you'll walk for half an hour in the middle of the day, or cycle to work. Maybe you'll look at the sort of food you eat, resolve to take a break for lunch and spend a few minutes or even half an hour away from the patients, the wards and the computer.

Stop neglecting your own needs to care for your body, mind and spirit in whatever ways are good for you. Right now, you may have forgotten how important it is and skip meals, not taking much exercise, being at work for long hours and then worrying about patients when you are away from work, forgetting to holidays or spending quality time with your friends and family. You never go out into nature, by the ocean, or walk in woods, or even spend time in parks watching birds and animals.

Hobbies have become something from the past and you remember vaguely how you used to love playing music or painting or reading novels. Everything is Medicine.

It doesn't have to be like that. When you decide to care for yourself more, start today with something simple. This might be to go for a walk, even around the hospital grounds, or away from your Surgery for a while. Once you start a new habit, you can gradually increase how much you do.

Look at what you eat and drink and make a small change: less alcohol, more fruit and vegetables. But don't be vague - say you are going to have an apple with your breakfast each day, for example. Be specific and make healthy changes one bite at a time.

Equally important is time in nature, time for you to relax, be calm and do things you love to do outside of Medicine.

You are constantly caring for others and helping them to lead healthy lives. But have you been prioritising your own self-care?

It is essential for you to take care of yourself to provide the best care possible for your patients.

Here are a few tips to improve your self-care:

Set boundaries and learn to say no. Prioritise your own health and wellbeing by not over-committing yourself to work or other obligations.

- Eat well: You know the importance of a healthy diet. Make sure you are eating plenty of fruits, vegetables, and lean proteins.

- Exercise regularly: Exercise is not only good for your physical health but also for your mental health. Try to incorporate physical activity into your daily routine.
- Practice self-reflection: Take time to reflect on your own emotions and thoughts. This may involve journalling or talking with a therapist.
- Take breaks: It's okay to take breaks throughout the day to recharge. This could be as simple as taking a few deep breaths or going for a short walk.

Caring for yourself will better equip you to care for your patients. Make self-care a priority in your life.

25. Decide what you really want.

Deciding can be a challenge because you wonder if what you've decided is right. These tips will enable you to decide and have a back-up choice if it turns out you need it!

While you are deliberating about deciding, become clearer of what your choices are because sometimes things aren't just a matter of choice A or choice B, there may be a midway choice C which can take good things from the other choices and find a compromise that you hadn't considered.

If you seem to have an enormous number of choices, start by grouping them together as broad solutions rather than very specific at this stage. When you decide the category of your desired choice, you will then be better able to narrow your choice more easily.

When you've decided on the main type of choice to make, then you can chunk down into smaller choices and get into greater specifics about exactly what you want to do. When you do, you can then ask yourself what it is you now need to find out or learn about each choice before you make the final decision.

Make a list of pros and cons of each choice is a common way to decide, and it means that you will make an informed choice. However, not everyone decides in the same way; some seek advice from others with similar experiences, while others rely on intuition. Most of us use a bit of each of these.

Notice your internal voice as you write each pro and con if you are someone who decides on your internal feelings about something. You notice that as you write each word, you will feel something slightly different and, using this aspect of your own physiology, you can make an assessment of what choice to make.

Go along with your 'gut feeling' about the right choice to make because this will help you choose as much as any other parameter such as hearing what people say and what you want to do, or looking at photos or objects connected with what you plan to do. Each of these are ways in which people decide. We all use a bit of each, but many of us have a preponderance.

If your primary choice goes completely wrong, prepare a Plan B to avoid having no alternative. Although you can't be sure that the choice you make will be the best choice for you, it is always re-assuring to know that if your first choice fails that you can fall back on another choice.

Assuming you have finally made a choice which you can refer to as Plan A, then be as prepared for all eventualities as you can. Prepare more detail for your plan A: is there anything you need to find out before you can be sure it's right for you?

When you know what you really want, you will be more able to tell others and no longer have to put up with what you no longer want. It's easy to have vague goals, but when you make your goals specific, then you are much more likely to achieve them. So, instead of 'I can't go on like this: I feel stressed all the time and don't think I can cope with this workload very much longer,' define what would make a difference. Imagine being calm and getting through your workload in a relaxed and efficient way.

Explore ways you could change from stress and overwhelm to satisfaction and order. What one change could make a tremendous difference? Start with something small and achievable. For example, arriving at work thirty minutes earlier would give you the chance to catch up with correspondence and urgent requests. But don't stop there. Ask yourself what you need to do to get there earlier: maybe set your alarm or pack your bag for work the night before, or decide which clothes to wear the next day, before you go to bed.

Whatever you decide, ask yourself what do you need to do to achieve that? This will bring you to the very first easy step that will set the ball rolling towards your big goal, less stressed and more relaxed. This process enables your big goals to be realised in small chunks, step by step, as you change your life for the better.

26. Communicate clearly.

When you are about to change how you do something, you may need to explain to others around you why you are about to behave differently. If you make a dramatic change by either stopping doing something you've been doing for ages or start doing something you haven't done before, tell the others that they may notice something different about you from such-and-such a time or day.

Improve your communication with those affected by your behavioural changes. Too many people don't get as far as talking about what they would like to do because they assume that so and so would be upset or not approve. That might be true, but you won't know their reaction until you do that thing. By communicating your intentions, you will help to prepare that person for what you intend to do.

First and most important is to get into rapport with the other person. This means getting into a connection with that person so they really hear what you are telling them. This can involve:

◈ Speaking to them at a time for their full attention.

◈ Making sure they are listening to you.

◈ Being on the same physical level as them (e.g. both of you sitting, or both of you standing up).

If you think they may not like what you are going to say, start with something positive, then tell them the main thing positively, and finish with something definitely positive from their point of view.

If people don't seem to hear or understand what you say, learn to:

◈ Listen twice as much as you speak. (Two ears and one mouth!)

◈ Try to really understand their point of view because when you show understanding to them, then they are more likely to give you the attention and consideration you want.

Give a positive feedback sandwich if you are not happy with the way someone is behaving. Say something complimentary, then say what you really want; finally end on something positive. You should be an excellent communicator, but it's not always easy to say what you really want to say, especially if it might upset the other person. This applies when dealing with patients as much as with friends and colleagues.

If you want to say 'no', do so without ambiguity. Say 'no' don't say 'maybe later' or I'll need to think about that'. However, you can start with 'thank you for thinking of me', then say 'I'm sorry I can't do what you want,' and end with 'I appreciate you asking me.'

The feedback sandwich is like a hamburger bun: something white and fluffy (the bun), then something meaty, followed by more fluffiness. Fluffiness means saying something positive and, if possible, complimentary. Saying this when you start the conversation means that the other person will be more responsive to the next bit when you follow the positive bit with 'however....' and tell them the bit that you want to let them know but they may not want to hear. After that, finish with something positive.

Clear communication is essential. Patients rely on you to interpret their symptoms and provide them with proper diagnosis and treatment plans. Therefore, it is imperative to communicate clearly, whether it be with your patients, nurses, or other healthcare professionals.

MEET THE CHALLENGES OF WORKING AS A DOCTOR

Here are a few things to keep in mind when communicating with others:

Use simple language: Medical jargon can be confusing and overwhelming for patients. Use simple language that patients can understand and avoid using technical terms.

- Be concise: Get to the point quickly and avoid rambling. Patients may not have the attention span or ability to remember everything you say.
- Listen actively: Listen carefully to your patients' concerns and ask clarifying questions. This shows that you care about their health and are taking their concerns seriously.
- Be empathetic: Patients want to feel like they are being heard and that their health concerns matter. Show empathy and understanding towards their situation.
- Repeat important information your patients need to remember, such as medication dosages, treatment plans, and follow-up appointments.

Effective communication is essential in building trust and ensuring that patients receive the best possible care. By communicating clearly, you can make a positive impact on your patients' lives.

27. Be responsible for yourself.

There are many times in your life when you must stop and ask yourself: 'What shall I do now?' in relation to your career path or to your personal life. This is the doctor's dilemma.

It may seem difficult to make that decision because you are so engulfed in the 'what will people think of me if I do this rather than that?' mindset. There may be well-meaning senior colleagues who talk as if they know what sort of life is best for you and, as they describe how they see your future, you inwardly cringe and wonder how they could believe that they know what you really want.

No-one can foretell what the future will bring for you. That is why making some decisions about your life is such a problem for many doctors. However, when you say or thinking like: 'if I had my time over again, I would definitely have made a different choice,' then you have a strong clue about what you could or even should do with your life now.

Think back to a time when you took a leap into the unknown or did something scary and recall what gave you the push to do it. Maybe you took a deep breath and jumped or maybe you wanted to prove someone's judgement about you was wrong. You took that apprehension and just did it.

Since you have thought about alternatives and other possibilities about your life, you have already started on a journey of change and even with your dilemma about which path to take, it's important to make a choice without endlessly procrastinating. Even if you decide to stay where you are, things will be different because you have been considering other possibilities. That means that something will have changed in your present situation, too. You may have discovered a way to improve it or may become more determined than ever to explore new ways. Project your thoughts into the future perhaps a year or several years ahead and imagine your life if you continue as you are or if you make the changes you are considering.

You can't always be responsible for the way others deal with the things you do. You may avoid change because you don't want to upset someone.

The key is to find a solution that benefits both of you. It's natural to worry about how your nearest and dearest will react if you change your life.

It's important to tell them what you are going to do, allow them the chance to react in their own way, and then deal with it. It can be useful if you point out the advantages to them of your changes.

Sometimes people close to you react negatively to your plan because they feel 'let down' or 'cheated' by you. However, it is not the way to live your life, to only do things predetermined or decided by others.

An example of this in the medical profession is being told which jobs to apply for to reach consultant status even though that may not be what you want to achieve, or you may not want those jobs.

As a medical professional, you play a crucial role in saving lives and promoting good health. However, it is equally important that you take responsibility for your own well-being, too.

Your job can be stressful, with long hours and high risks. It is important that you maintain a healthy work-life balance, take time off when needed, and prioritise self-care. This can involve not only exercise and a healthy diet but also seeking mental health support.

MEET THE CHALLENGES OF WORKING AS A DOCTOR

It is vital that you always behave with honesty and professionalism. This means acting ethically, avoiding conflicts of interest, and keeping up with best practices and medical research.

Self-care is making sure there is less avoidable stress. If you drive to work, be sure you have enough fuel for the journey. Try to use a route to avoid lengthy hold ups.

Consider other ways to travel. If it's practical, cycle and get your daily exercise done without too much extra time taken in your day.

If you travel by train or bus, use the time to think or catch up with reading, either journal reading or a novel.

Ultimately, your responsibility to your patients and your profession begins with responsibility to yourself. By taking care of yourself, you can better serve those who depend on you for their health and well-being.

28. Discover a prescription for change.

Imagine having your day sorted so well that you have enough time to

have a lunch break

- exercise
- spend time with your family and friends
- enjoy life

Picture how your work-life balance improves and how you become more organised.

Map out exactly what steps you need to take to get your life transformed as quickly as possible, what you can do to look after yourself so you can deal with whatever stress and frustration your work throws at you.

Avoid making the same mistakes many doctors make in relation to managing their lives.

You can do it when you find your personal prescription for change!

You are in a unique position to prescribe change for yourself. Because you help others, you understand the importance of self-care. Here are some suggestions for discovering your own prescription for change:

Take time for self-reflection. Before you can make any changes, you need to be clear on the areas that require improvement. Take some time to reflect on your life and career and identify any areas where you feel stuck or unfulfilled.

- Set achievable goals. Once you've identified the areas that need improvement, set realistic goals that help you make progress in that direction. Make sure that these goals are achievable, measurable, and timed.

- Build a support network. Making changes is never easy, and having people around you who support and encourage you can make an enormous difference. Reach out to family, friends, and colleagues who can offer you helpful feedback and advice.

- Prioritise self-care. You spend a lot of time taking care of others. However, it's important to prioritise self-care so that you can stay healthy and avoid burnout. Get enough rest, eat well, and exercise regularly.

- Embrace learning. Medicine is constantly developing, and it's important to stay up-to-date with the latest research and techniques. Seek opportunities for continuing education or explore new areas that interest you.

By following these tips, you can come up with a prescription for change that empowers you to take control of your life and career. Good luck on your journey of self-discovery and growth!

29. Celebrate your wins.

It's time to celebrate all that you have achieved. You have dedicated your time and energy to improving the health and well-being of your patients. You have spent countless hours studying and learning your skills, and your efforts have not gone unnoticed.

Your expertise and knowledge have helped overcome some of the world's most challenging health issues, from tackling new diseases to developing innovative treatments and cures. Through your work, you have saved lives and improved the quality of life for so many others.

The path can often feel overwhelming, filled with long hours, challenging cases, and the emotional weight of the responsibilities you carry.

However, amidst the hectic schedules and constant demands, take a moment to celebrate the victories, big and small, that shape your professional journey. Here's how to do that:

Reflect on your achievements. Look back at what you've accomplished. Whether it's mastering a complex procedure, successfully diagnosing a challenging case, or simply building strong relationships with patients, each success contributes to your growth as a physician. Keep a journal to document these successes. It will be a source of motivation during tough times.

Create a celebration tradition. This could be as simple as treating yourself to a favourite meal, scheduling a spa day, or planning a fun outing with friends or family. Whatever it is, make it a point to acknowledge your hard work and dedication.

Share your successes. Whether it's through a casual chat or a more formal setting like a team meeting, discussing your achievements can lead to a supportive environment and inspire others to share their successes as well.

Recognise team efforts. Acknowledge the contributions of your team members, from nurses and administrative staff to specialists and residents. Celebrating collective achievements not only boosts morale but also strengthens teamwork.

Welcome patient gratitude. One of the most rewarding aspects of being a doctor is the effect you have on your patients' lives. When a patient expresses their gratitude or shares their success story, take a moment to celebrate that emotional victory. It's a powerful reminder of why you chose this profession.

Set new goals. Celebration is a perfect time to set new goals. Outline what you want to accomplish next in your career. This creates a continuous cycle of growth and success.

Practice mindfulness. Taking a moment to pause and appreciate your journey affects your well-being. Practise meditation, yoga, or simply taking a deep breath and appreciating the moment can serve as a reminder of the good work you do.

30. Finally.

Hopefully you are now better equipped to meet the challenges you face as a doctor.

Working as a doctor is a extremely rewarding yet demanding profession that requires strength, compassion, and solid dedication. As you experience the difficulties of healthcare, you face a multitude of challenges that test your skills, knowledge, and emotional strength. Here are key qualities and tactics that help you meet these challenges effectively:

Flexibility: The ability to bounce back from setbacks and adapt to changing circumstances is crucial. You face unpredictable situations daily, from emergency cases to changing healthcare regulations. Building strength can involve mindfulness practices, seeking support from colleagues, and maintaining a balanced life outside of work.

Effective communication is vital. You must clearly convey complex medical information, listen actively to patients' concerns, and work collaboratively with healthcare teams.

Understanding the emotional and psychological needs of patients is essential. Showing empathy can help build trust and improve patient satisfaction. You can improve your empathetic skills through reflective practices

Continuous learning: The medical field is ever-changing, with new research, techniques, and technologies emerging regularly. Committing to lifelong learning through continuing education, workshops, and professional development ensures you remain at the forefront of medical knowledge and innovation.

Strong problem-solving skills: You often need to think critically and make quick decisions under pressure. Developing strong analytical and problem-solving skills is vital for diagnosing conditions and determining the best possible treatment plans.

Time management: Balancing patient care, administrative duties, and personal time can be challenging. Effective time management strategies, such as prioritising tasks and setting realistic goals, can help you maintain productivity while maintaining your well-being.

Self-care: The demanding nature of being a doctor can lead to burnout if self-care is neglected. Establishing healthy habits—such as regular exercise, proper nutrition, and sufficient rest—can increase both personal health and professional performance.

Building a strong professional network can provide support and resources. Co-operating with other healthcare professionals encourages an environment of shared knowledge and collective problem-solving, ultimately improving patient care.

In conclusion, the ability to meet the challenges of working as a doctor lies in encouraging flexibility, communication, empathy, and continuous growth. By accent self-care and collaboration, you can thrive in your profession and provide the best care possible for your patients.

It's easy to focus solely on the challenges. However, by deliberately taking the time to celebrate your wins, you not only improve your well-being, but you also inspire those around you. Success isn't just about the end goal, it's about recognising and appreciating the journey that leads you there. Take a moment today to celebrate you!

Follow the suggestions made in this book, so you can meet the challenges of working as a doctor and lead the life you truly want!

Don't miss out!

Visit the website below and you can sign up to receive emails whenever Susan Kersley publishes a new book. There's no charge and no obligation.

https://books2read.com/r/B-A-EFNC-TFDKC

BOOKS 2 READ

Connecting independent readers to independent writers.

Did you love *Meet the Challenges of Working as a Doctor*? Then you should read *Prescription for Change*[1] by Susan Kersley!

This book is a catalyst for doctors to have the life they want. It promotes a healthy work life balance and is a practical easy to read guide with useful tips and advice for doctors to be less stressed and enjoy life more. Written by Susan Kersley a retired doctor who worked in the N.H.S for thirty years. This book is for doctors who wonder if they can continue working in Medicine and want to discover ways to make their lives happier and more balanced.

Read more at https://susankersley.co.uk.

---

1. https://books2read.com/u/brDOkm

2. https://books2read.com/u/brDOkm

About the Author

Susan Kersley has written personal development and self-help books for doctors and others, and books about retirement and novels.

She was a doctor for thirty years and then left Medicine to be a Life Coach..

Now retired, she is updating her books and writing more. Please visit her website https://susankersley.co.uk

If you enjoyed this book, **please take a moment to leave a review.** Reviews are so important for independent authors.

Read more at https://susankersley.co.uk.